THE VISION:
REFLECTIONS ON THE WAY OF THE SOUL

Poet, philosopher and artist, Kahlil Gibran was born near Mount Lebanon. The millions of Arabic-speaking peoples familiar with his writings in that language consider him the genius of his age, but his fame and influence spread far beyond the Near East. His poetry has been translated into more than twenty languages and his drawings and paintings have been exhibited all over the world. His many works include *The Prophet*, his masterpiece of religious inspiration; *The Garden of the Prophet; The Storm: Stories and Prose Poems; The Beloved: Reflections on the Path of the Heart; Jesus: The Son of Man;* and *The Voice of Kahlil Gibran*, an anthology of his writings. All of these are published in Penguin Arkana. He was for many years the leader of a Lebanese literary circle in New York, where he died in 1931.

Juan R. I. Cole is Professor of Modern Middle Eastern and South Asian History at the University of Michigan. He has served as Director of that University's Center for Middle Eastern and North African Studies, and on the Joint Committee for the Near and Middle East of the Social Science Research Council. He has authored, edited or translated numerous books about the Middle East and the Muslim world, an area he has been studying for a quarter of a century. He spent six years in the Arab world, and has also lived in Ethiopia, India and Pakistan.

Robin Waterfield was educated at the universities of Manchester and Cambridge. He has been a university lecturer, and both copy-editor and commissioning editor for Penguin. He is now a self-employed writer and consultant editor, and his publications range from academic articles and translations of Greek philosophical texts to children's fiction.

THE VISION

REFLECTIONS ON THE WAY OF THE SOUL

Translated by Juan R. I. Cole,
with a new introduction by Robin Waterfield

Kahlil Gibran

ARKANA

PENGUIN BOOKS

ARKANA

Published by the Penguin Group
Penguin Books Ltd, 27 Wrights Lane, London w8 5tz, England
Penguin Books USA Inc., 375 Hudson Street, New York, New York 10014, USA
Penguin Books Australia Ltd, Ringwood, Victoria, Australia
Penguin Books Canada Ltd, 10 Alcorn Avenue, Toronto, Ontario, Canada m4v 3b2
Penguin Books (NZ) Ltd, 182–190 Wairau Road, Auckland 10, New Zealand

Penguin Books Ltd, Registered Offices: Harmondsworth, Middlesex, England

First published in the USA by White Cloud Press 1994
Published in Penguin Books 1997
1 3 5 7 9 10 8 6 4 2

Illustration credits
All illustrations by Kahlil Gibran: Unity of Religions, from *Al-Mawákib*, p. 4;
Kneeling figure, p. 32; Lute player, p. 49; The Spirit of Light, p. 85; Mother Earth, p. 100.

Set in 11/15pt Postscript Monotype Perpetua
Typeset by Rowland Phototypesetting Ltd, Bury St Edmunds, Suffolk
Printed in England by Clays Ltd, St Ives plc

CONTENTS

CONTENTS

INTRODUCTION
to the Penguin Edition

With all due acknowledgement to the pioneering work of earlier translators of Gibran, it is perfectly clear that it is only with this new series of translations, first published in North America by White Cloud Press, that we can begin to appreciate Gibran's early Arabic work properly. At last we see why he is so famous throughout the Arabic world for the profundity and lucidity of his thought and expression. Here is no well-meaning earnestness but the lightness and clarity of youth seeking urgently to get its message across; here is no heavy-handed learner but an acute and penetrating mind, and a deft artist.

We can go further. I will almost say that there is material in these early works which rivals his best-known work, *The Prophet*, in profundity. Or if that appears to some to be an exaggeration, let me at least have this point – that Gibran's early Arabic works *reveal* the profundity of *The Prophet*. For some have tried to dismiss the pithy nature of *The Prophet* as the display of a mind that was unsure of itself, and so was reluctant to express its convictions in an argued form, but

preferred the superficiality of paradox and apophthegm. However, a good read of the Arabic works which precede *The
Prophet* and his other English-language writings shows how
much background these later works have. There are years of
profound thought and reflection laid bare here, which are
assumed, implicit, in the English works.

The fame of *The Prophet* is such that it has eclipsed these
earlier works and made people think that Gibran was a
one-book wonder. This is far from being the case. Gibran
only began to write books in English at the end of the 1910s,
by which time he had already had an illustrious career as an
Arabic man of letters, was renowned throughout the Arabic
world, and had helped to launch a revolution in Arabic
literature.

Born in 1883, Gibran emigrated with most of his family
to the States in 1895 and settled in Boston for a while,
before returning for a few years to what is now Lebanon to
complete his education. Throughout his childhood he had
been attracted equally to both the writer's pen and the artist's
pencil, but it was initially as a promising artist that he came
to the attention of members of Boston's *fin de siècle* set
(especially the professional eccentric and gentleman photo-
grapher Fred Holland Day). However, by the time he came
back to Boston after completing his education in 1902, he
had already begun to experiment with writing. He continued
to draw and paint: he attended the Academy Julian in Paris
for a couple of years from 1908 to 1910, and always worked
hard at his paintings, but from the time his first published
work appeared (a short monograph on music, published in

New York in Arabic in 1905) he attracted attention as a writer.

There was a thriving Arabic literary scene in the United States. Perhaps surprisingly, there were literally dozens of Arabic-language journals and newspapers being published for the immigrant population – more proportionately than for any other immigrant group – and particularly for the Lebanese Syrians, who were generally speaking better educated than many of their fellow Arabs. Although many of these newspapers were shortlived, a number of them lasted longer and served as important vehicles for both political and literary movements, and their readership extended from New York to other immigrant groups in South America and Australia, and back home to Syria and Egypt. By the 1920s the first generation of immigrants was beginning to become assimilated, and their children were native Americans, so English-language Arabic papers began to take over from their Arabic precursors – but by then Gibran's fame in the Arabic-speaking world was already assured.

He began by writing incidental pieces, but was soon given his own column, entitled 'Tears and Laughter', in 1906, in the paper al-Mohajer (The Immigrant), published in New York. This newspaper was also the publisher of his earliest Arabic books. All the pieces in The Vision are taken from Gibran's Arabic newspaper writing, and we find many familiar themes contained in them.

For a start, like many young men, Gibran could be impatient with his fellow humans. Why could they not see that they were wasting their lives on illusions and pretensions?

[ix]

Why could they not sense the profound metaphysical distinction between appearance and reality? And, since Gibran himself felt that he did have clearer vision in these respects, he tended to separate himself from the rest of humankind, as one with a message – a poet, a prophet, an educator. We find this nest of themes in, for instance, 'The Anthem of Humanity', 'The Most Great Ocean' and 'The Voice of the Poet'.

But if this were all there were to Gibran's early thought, he would be indistinguishable from hundreds, perhaps thousands of cocksure young writers. There is more, however – a great deal more. In the first place, he is capable of placing himself squarely within the common mass of humankind, in that he shares their blindness and attachment to materiality, despite himself, despite the visions he has been granted by his soul. His impatience with the 'rest' of mankind is exactly echoed by his own soul's impatience with Gibran himself in 'Have Mercy, My Soul' and 'My Soul is Heavy Laden'. In 'Between Reality and Fantasy', there is less talk of *you* and more of *us*: Gibran himself is just as trapped, of course, in the human condition as anyone else.

Then again, to offset the strong influence of Nietzsche on the young Gibran in fostering his despair about the human condition, there is a strong vein of Whitmanesque optimism about the future destiny of humanity as a whole. Whitman had written in 'Song of the Open Road':

> Forever alive, forever forward,
> Stately, solemn, sad, withdrawn, baffled, mad, turbulent,
>   feeble, dissatisfied,

Desperate, proud, fond, sick, accepted by men, rejected by
men,

They go! they go! I know that they go, but I know not where
they go,

But I know that they go toward the best – toward something
great.

And Gibran echoes just this in 'The Anthem of Humanity',
'Children of Gods, Scions of Apes' and 'Perfection'.

In any case, as Gibran reminds himself in 'The Visit of
Wisdom', 'The person you consider ignorant and insignificant
is the one who came from God, that he might learn bliss
from grief and knowledge from gloom' (p. 43). Or again,
'Whoso does not see travails can never gaze on joy' (p. 79);
or again, the 'good counsel' his soul gives him in the poem
of that title is to find in everything, however mundane or
disregarded, something that affirms life, love and hope.

There are other familiar themes in this book – reincar-
nation, the importance of love and beauty, the celebration
of poverty, the Romantic fascination with death; more
unusually, since Gibran was a serious-minded young man,
there are nice touches of humour in 'The Philosophy of
Logic'. But I have concentrated on Nietzschean gloom not
just because it was a strong trait in the early Gibran, but also
because the fact that it is counteracted at the same time as
being professed shows how hard it is to pigeonhole Gibran.
He was above all else a poet, an artist, and art is never simple.
If it had a simple, rational message to convey, it would not
choose painting or poetry as its medium, but the discursive

treatise. As Gibran himself says in this volume, 'Art is a step from what is obvious and well-known toward what is arcane and concealed' (p. 58); and 'Art lies in the silent, pulsating intervals between the high notes and the low notes. It lies in the feeling that steals into you from listening to an ode . . . It lies in the picture's revelation to you, so that you see, while you are gazing at it, what transcends and is more beautiful than it' (p. 75). So if Gibran was an artist, he was trying to convey feelings rather than a coherent philosophy. Very often his work is like one of those Japanese paper flowers which expand when added to the water of one's attention – and from a single stem several blossoms may grow on further readings of the same piece.

The second piece in this book, which gives its title to the volume as a whole, may serve as a kind of manifesto for much of Gibran's Arabic writing: 'Life without love is like a tree without blossoms or fruit . . . Life without rebellion is like the seasons without spring . . . Life without liberty is like a body without spirit' (p. 8). This is not the place to go in detail into Gibran's lifelong participation, even at a distance, in his native country's painful and often bloody struggle to emerge as an independent unit from the death throes of the old Ottoman Empire, nor into his constant scornful rejection of anything that smacked of tyranny, however noble or even religious the cause in the name of which the common people were being oppressed. Suffice it to say, while avoiding the trap of trying to pigeonhole Gibran, that these three issues (love, rebellion and liberty) with their concomitants (beauty, truth and thought) constitute the energy, so to speak, that gives life to the forms and themes of Gibran's work.

It was certainly as an artist as well as a thinker that Gibran was known in the Arabic world. Not only was he an early, and a particularly forceful, proponent of ideas such as personal liberty, but he was at the forefront of a literary revolution which has had a permanent effect. Classical and neo-classical Arabic writing was caught in a mire of strict adherence to form. Freed from this by the physical distance of North America as much as by the spirit of the times, Gibran and a few other young writers began to experiment with different forms and themes. He allowed himself greater latitude in his vocabulary and figures of speech; he experimented with using more than one metre per poem; above all, he and others such as Ameen Rihani developed the prose poem as an Arabic form. Prose poetry may be defined as prose with poetic emotion and rhythm; Gibran took it over from, especially, Whitman and perfected its form in Arabic. In short, Gibran played a crucially important part in initiating the Romantic revolution in Arabic literature, in shifting it from the safe ground of craftsmanship to dangerous waters of inspiration and imagination. And this revolution was speeded on its way by the pieces contained in this and its companion volumes.

Robin Waterfield

INTRODUCTION

Some 62 years after the passing of the poet and artist known as 'the man from Lebanon,' we have the opportunity to review afresh the creative talents and artistic accomplishments of Kahlil Gibran. The new translations now available through White Cloud Press enable us to better appreciate the modernity of his thought and the originality of his style.

Gibran arrived on Ellis Island from the Ottoman territory of Lebanon on June 25, 1895, a boy of 12 years. He grew to adulthood in Boston during a period when America's optimism was swelling as it broadened its cultural horizons and entered the international arena as a major political and economic power. Gibran's family, prompted by a family crisis, had left Mt. Lebanon seeking refuge from its economic privations and political turmoil.

In both the United States and the countries of the eastern Mediterranean, cherished cultural values were being challenged by the needs of a modern world. Young Kahlil bridged two very different cultures, drew from the riches of each, and made unique contributions to both.

In Boston, New York, and Paris he kept company with some of the leading artists and writers of the day. An outstanding artist himself, his captivating portraits include Mary Haskell, Fred Holland Day, Josephine Peabody (his early mentors and friends), W. B. Yeats, Auguste Rodin, 'Abdu'l-Baha, the spiritual leader of the Baha'i faith, and many other outstanding figures.

Gibran's Arabic writings attracted a great deal of attention in Egypt, Syria, and Lebanon. He became one of the most acclaimed and most controversial Arabic writers in the Middle East during the first third of the twentieth century, though he wrote from Boston and New York. His book *Spirits Rebellious* was condemned, banned, and burned in Lebanon.

To his English readers he offered images of the serene, natural beauty of his native home and the symbols and ideas of a rich mystical heritage. Most of Gibran's English readers are familiar with him as the mystic, the sage, and the storyteller. These were roles he played out like the roles he asked his models to take when he painted. Through these personas he shared his artistic vision that he hoped would change the outlook of his readers.

The Vision contains excellent examples of Gibran speaking as the critical sage ('My Soul Gave Me Good Counsel'), the inspired poet ('The Poet of Baalbek'), and the religious visionary ('The Anthem of Humanity'). Many of his stories and prose poems contain traces of the painful experiences of his impoverished childhood in the village of Bisharri, overshadowed by the majestic beauty of Mt. Lebanon (fine examples of these stories are found in *The Storm*, translated by John Walbridge and *Spirit Brides* translated by Juan Cole). He suffused his vivid descriptions of the pastoral landscape of that region with a love for beauty, serenity, and order. In that imaginative experience he sought refuge and a resolution to the suffering, conflict, and injustice he experienced in human society.

The Vision includes several examples of this approach, particularly 'The Most Great Ocean,' 'The Visit of Wisdom,' and 'Beauty.' These provide fine examples of the Romantic sensibility that contrasts an idealized natural world to the banal corruption of human endeavors.

While to some, Romanticism represents sentimental indulgence and a preoccupation with the idealized beauties of the natural world, Gibran, like most Romantic writers and artists, developed his art in rebellion against the rigid standards and forms of the Classical aesthetic. This artistic revolt pitted the individual against the larger framework of social norms and values. Gibran vigorously criticized the ugliness, injustice, and staleness of Syrian and Lebanese society, implying a broader criticism of Middle Eastern society. His critique is evident in many of his writings, though particularly poignant in the stories 'Marta al-Baniya' and 'Yuhanna the Madman' found in *Spirit Brides*.

Gibran did not confine his challenge to Arabic culture. He sought out the universal elements in his specific experience to formulate a general critique of human society, concentrating on the hypocrisy of its religious institutions, the injustice of its political institutions, and the narrow outlook of its citizenry, whom he viewed as both victims of, and participants in, the oppression generated by these institutions.

If we read his English works, *The Forerunner*, *The Madman*, and *The Prophet* as a trilogy we can see how Gibran intertwined the roles of seeker, rebel, and prophet into a single approach. Human society can be transformed through the process of envisioning the ideal potentials of human beings while identifying their shortcomings (*The Forerunner*), destruction of all that is corrupt and evil (*The Madman*), then building the ideal society based on universal, non-sectarian principles of love, compassion, justice, understanding, beauty, and recognition of humanity as a universal family (*The Prophet*).

To his Arabic readers Gibran offered an entirely new concept of Arabic poetry. He broke away from the constraints of traditional forms and standards for poetic expression that had been adhered to for more than one thousand years. He stressed the importance of individual creativity and independent thought. His poetic diction relied more on the rhythms and vocabulary of natural speech rather than the high rhetoric of classical poetry and its strict formal requirements. Instead he advocated the notion of organic form in Arabic poetry, arising internally from the poem's idea, its themes, and emotions, rather than dictated by extrinsic standards. He joined with several other Syrian writers living in America who held similar views and became the leading figure in the Pen Association, which included two other outstanding contributors to modern Arabic literature, Mikhail Naimy and Amin al-Rihani. This literary group had more impact on Arabic literature than the Bloomsbury group had on English literature and were responsible for introducing Romanticism into Arabic literature. Gibran more than any Arabic writer before or after him embodied the group's ideals and realized its aims in his published works.

Gibran developed his vision through an individual process of search and discovery. He was a self-educated man who integrated diverse theories and approaches, never accepting or submitting to a single discipline or religious affiliation. While Eastern Christianity exercised a strong influence on his ideas and beliefs, his interpretation was unique and antithetical to the ecclesiastics of his day. He freely incorporated folklore and ancient Middle Eastern mythologies, evident in *Spirit Brides*. He was also strongly influenced by American Transcendentalism, particularly the works of Emerson, as well as by European philosophy, especially Nietzsche. He shaped these diverse influences into a unified vision through his remarkable talents and independence of thought, due in large measure to his experience as an Arab immigrant to the United States. As a result he has made a lasting contribution to two cultures. Though both regions in their mutual conflicts have suffered greatly, perhaps in the life and works of this uniquely talented man we can find one span in the bridge between them.

Brian Miller

NOTE ON TEXTS

The pieces translated in this collection are taken from Mikhail Naimy, ed., *Al-majmu'ah al-kamilah li-mu'allafat Jibran Khalil Jibran*, Beirut, 1961, and were originally published in various Arabic journals and newspapers. They are: 'Nashid al-insan,' p. 343; 'Ru'ya,' pp. 415–416; 'al-Malik as-sajin,' pp. 375–376; 'al-Bahr al-a'zam,' pp 537–538; 'Sawt ash-sha'ir,' pp. 344–348; 'al-Jamal,' pp. 260–261; 'Abna' al-alihah wa ahfad al-qurud,' pp. 396–398; 'Rahmaki ya nafs rahmaki,' pp. 268–269; 'Nafsi muthqalah bi athmariha,' pp. 499–500; 'Ziyarat al-hikmah,' pp. 275–276; 'ash-Sha'ir al-Ba'labakki,' pp. 472–476; 'Bayn al-haqiqah wa al-khayal,' p. 280; 'Hafnah min rimal ash-shati',' pp. 501–502; 'Khalili,' pp. 310–311; 'Falsafat al-mantiq,' pp. 434–436; 'ash-Sha'ir,' pp. 316–317; 'al-Qushur wa al-lubab,' pp. 495–498; 'Anshudat az-zahrah,' p. 342; 'Ru'ya,' pp. 264–266; 'Wa'azatni nafsi,' pp. 516–519; 'Jamal al-mawt,' pp. 335–337; 'al-Huruf an-nariyyah,' pp. 261–262; 'Bayt as-sa'adah,' p. 298.

TRANSLATOR'S
ACKNOWLEDGEMENTS

This volume collects Gibran's major prose poems having to do with the spiritual life. Ethical and spiritual concerns are at the heart of much of Gibran's writing, including his classic, *The Prophet*, and it is hoped that readers will profit from having these pieces assembled in one book. Experts in modern Arabic literature have long remarked that previous translations into English of Kahlil Gibran's works were marred by many inadequacies of accuracy and of style. Although the idea of retranslating his Arabic works into contemporary English was my own, the notion of doing so as a set of thematic anthologies came from my dear friend John Walbridge. The latter was also kind enough to make a number of fruitful suggestions about which prose poems should be included in this volume, and without his wisdom and encouragement these new renderings might well not exist. I dedicate this translation to John, *nafs zakiyyah*.

Also indispensable have been the support and suggestions of Steven Scholl, publisher and founder of White Cloud

Press. As always, my wife Shahin provided many insightful observations, and her enthusiasm for this project was essential.

Juan R. I. Cole
Ann Arbor, Michigan
January 1994

THE VISION

THE ANTHEM OF
HUMANITY

'You were dead, and He revived you;
then He will cause you to die, and
He will revive you; then unto
Him shall ye return.'
The Qur'an, 2:26

I have existed from all eternity and, behold, I am here; and I shall exist till the end of time, for my being has no end.

I soared into limitless space and took wing in the imaginal world, approaching the circle of exalted light; and here I am now, mired in matter.

I listened to the teachings of Confucius, imbibed the wisdom of Brahma, and sat beside Buddha beneath the tree of insight. And now I am here, wrestling with ignorance and unbelief. I was on Sinai when Yahweh shed His effulgence on Moses; at the River Jordan I witnessed the miracles of the Nazarene; and in Medina I heard the words of the Messenger to the Arabs. And here I am now, a captive of confusion. I beheld the might of Babylon, the glory of Egypt, and the grandeur of Greece; and I still see the weakness, degradation, and pettiness in all those works. I sat with the sorcerers of Endor, the seers of Assyria, the prophets of Palestine; and I persist in singing the truth. I memorized the wisdom revealed to India, the heartfelt odes wrought by the inhabitants of the Arabian peninsula, and the music that

embodies the sentiments of the Western people: yet still I am blind and do not see, deaf and do not hear. I endured the brutality of grasping conquerors, suffered oppression at the hands of tyrannical rulers, and was enslaved by despots: yet a power remains whereby I struggle against the days.

I saw and heard all that while still a child, and shall see and hear the exploits of youth and their consequences; then I shall grow old, and achieve perfection, and return unto God.

I existed from all eternity and, behold, I am here; and I shall exist till the end of time, for my being has no end.

THE VISION

When night fell and slumber draped its mantle over the face of the earth, I left my bed and walked toward the sea, saying to myself, 'The sea sleeps not. And in the wakefulness of the sea is a balm for the spirit that does not rest.'

I arrived at the shore, where the mists had rolled down from the mountain peaks and enveloped that locale the way a grey veil cloaks the face of a beautiful girl. I stood staring at the armies of waves, listening to their jubilant shouts, contemplating the eternal, clandestine powers that lay behind them – the powers that race with storms, rage alongside volcanoes, smile with the mouths of roses, and lilt with brooks.

After a little while I looked around to find three apparitions sitting on a nearby boulder, the mists concealing yet not concealing them. I walked slowly toward them, as if some force in their being attracted me and subdued my will.

When I had come within a few footsteps of them, I halted and stood staring at them fixedly, as though sorcery pervaded that place, blunting my determination and awakening the imagination latent in my spirit.

At that very moment one of the three arose and, in a voice that seemed to issue from the depths of the sea, he said, 'Life without love is like a tree without blossoms or fruit. Love without beauty is like flowers without fragrance and fruit without seeds . . . Life, love, and beauty – three persons in one substance, independent, absolute, accepting no change or separation.' Having spoken these words, he sat down again in the same place.

Then the second phantom stood and, in a voice like the roar of floodwaters, he said, 'Life without rebellion is like the seasons without spring. Rebellion without truth is like spring in a bleak, arid desert . . . Life, rebellion, and truth – three persons in one substance, accepting no separation or alteration.'

The third specter now gained his feet and, in a voice like a thunderclap, he said, 'Life without liberty is like a body without spirit. Liberty without thought is like a disturbed spirit . . . Life, liberty, and thought – three persons in one substance, eternal, never-ending, and unceasing.'

All three apparitions now arose, and with horrifying voices they said unanimously, 'Love and what generates it. Rebellion and what creates it. Liberty and what nourishes it. Three manifestations of God. And God is the conscience of the rational world.'

A silence fell then, replete with the rustling of unseen wings and the trembling of ethereal bodies. I closed my eyes, listening to the echo of the words I had heard. When I opened them and looked again, I saw only the sea, wrapped in a shroud of mist. I drew near to the boulder where the three apparitions had been sitting, and descried only a column of incense rising into the sky.

THE CAPTIVE KING

Take heart, O imprisoned sovereign, for your tribulations in your cell are no greater than mine in my body.

Lie down and resign yourself to your fate, O fearsome one. For to be perturbed in the face of vicissitudes befits jackals, and caged monarchs can acquit themselves well only by showing contempt for the dungeon and the jailer.

Quieten your alarm, O youth of high resolve, and look at me. For I subsist among the slaves of life as you subsist behind bars. What difference is there between us, save a restless dream that follows my soul but fears to come near you?

We are both exiled from our homelands, remote from our families and loved ones. Compose yourself and endure patiently, as I do, the torments of days and nights, ridiculing those weaklings who vanquished us by virtue of their numbers, not by means of their individual determination.

What good can come of visitors, clamor, and the deaf who hear not?

I shouted before you did in their ears, and caught the attention only of gloomy shades. Just as you did, I reviewed their ranks, and found none among them but cowards who wax bold and overbearing before those in chains, and weaklings who hold their heads high and affect severity before prisoners in their cells.

Gaze, mighty king, upon those who crowd around your prison now. Search their faces and you will find what you saw in the mien of the least of your subjects and courtiers in the trackless desert. Some are like rabbits in their faintness of heart; some are like foxes in their cunning; and some equal snakes in their vileness. But none has the blamelessness of a rabbit, the intelligence of a fox, or the wisdom of a serpent.

Look, that one is like a filthy pig, but his flesh cannot be eaten. That one resembles a coarse water buffalo, but his hide is useless. That one is like a dim-witted donkey, but walks on two legs. That one looks like an ill-omened raven, but sells his croaking in temples. That one is like a haughty, preening peacock, but his feathers are borrowed.

Gaze, dreaded emperor, upon these mansions and edifices, for they are cramped nests wherein live human beings who pride themselves on the ornamented ceilings that block their view of the stars. They delight in the solidity of the walls which hide them from the rays of the sun. These buildings are murky caves, in the shadow of which the blossoms of youth wither, in the corners of which the torch of love turns to ash, and in the air of which the traces of dreams dissolve into columns of smoke. They are bizarre subterranean vaults, wherein the child's cradle swings toward the couch of the deathly ill, while the bridal bed sits beside the bier of a corpse.

Look, glorious prisoner, look at those wide avenues and narrow alleyways, for they are valleys of peril for those who travel them, with thieves crouched at every turn and bandits concealed on every side. They are an arena of continual battle between one object of desire and another, onto which descend spirits at war, though they lack swords, wrestling and snapping at one another without fangs. Or they are, rather, a forest of fear wherein dwell animals of tame appearance, with perfumed tails and polished horns, who are governed not by survival of the fittest but by endurance of the wiliest and most cunning. Their customs are not attributable to the best and strongest but to the most base and dishonest. As for their kings, they are no lions the like of yourself but, rather, odd creatures who possess the beaks of vultures, the claws of hyenas, the tongues of scorpions, and the croaking voices of frogs.

My spirit be your sacrifice, O captive king, for I have stood with you a long time and have talked at too great a length. But the heart that has been dethroned empathizes with over-thrown monarchs, and the lonely, imprisoned soul takes delight in the company of lonesome prisoners. Make allowances for a youth who talks incessantly, preferring this amusement to eating itself, who imbibes thoughts instead of ale.

Until we meet again, O fearsome despot. Should it not be in this strange world, it will be in the world of specters, where the spirits of kings gather together with those of martyrs.

THE MOST GREAT
OCEAN

Yesterday — and how remote yesterday is, yet how near — I went with my soul to the most great ocean, to wash away with its waters the dust and mire of the earth that had clung to us.

When we reached the shore we searched for a vacant spot that would shield us from prying eyes.

While we two were walking along we looked up and, behold, a man was sitting on a dusty rock. He grasped in his hand a bag, from which he took fistful after fistful of salt which he cast into the ocean.

My soul said to me, 'That man is a cynic, who sees nothing of life but its shadow. A cynic is not worthy to lay eyes upon our naked bodies. Let us leave this place, since there is no way we can bathe here.'

We departed from that spot and walked on until we arrived at an inlet. There we discovered a man standing on a white stone, holding in his hand a jewel-studded box. He was taking from it cubes of sugar and tossing them into the ocean.

My soul said to me, 'This man is an optimist, who sees

good omens where none exist. Beware lest an optimist see our naked bodies.'

We began walking once more, until we happened upon a man standing near the shore, picking up dead fish and tenderly returning them to the ocean.

My soul said to me, 'This is a compassionate person, who attempts to resuscitate those already in their graves. Let us avoid him.'

We finally arrived at a place where we saw a man drawing his fantasies in the sand. The waves came and erased his sketches, but he kept on doing what he was doing, time and again.

My soul said to me, 'Here is a mystic who has set up in his imagination an idol to worship. Let us leave him and his affairs.'

We strolled on until we espied, near a placid bay, a man scooping the foam from the surface of the water and shaking it into a carnelian bowl.

My soul said to me, 'This is a dreamer, who weaves a robe from spider webs that he might array himself in it. He has no right to see our naked bodies.'

We resumed our trek, and abruptly we heard a voice shouting, 'This is the deep sea, this is the mighty, terrifying ocean.'

We searched for the speaker and beheld a man standing with his back to the ocean. He had placed a seashell over his ear and was listening to its rumbling.

My soul said to me, 'Let us go, for this is a materialist, who has turned his back on everything he cannot fathom and busies his essence with particulars that accord with his own premises.'

We walked on until we saw a man in a grassy place between the stones who had buried his head in the sand.

I said to my soul, 'Come, my soul, let us bathe here. For that man cannot see us.'

My soul shook her head, saying, 'No, a thousand times no. The one you see is the worst of all people. He is pious and pure and veils himself from the tragedy of life, so that life has hidden its joys from his soul.'

Then a profound sorrow appeared on the face of my soul. In a voice broken with bitterness, she said, 'Let us get away from this shore, for there is no sheltered, concealed spot here where we can bathe. And I will never agree to loose my golden tresses in this wind, or to bare my tender breasts to this void, or to disrobe and stand naked before this light.'

My soul and I departed from that great ocean, and began to seek for the most great ocean.

THE VOICE OF
THE POET

I

Power sows in the depths of my heart, and I reap and gather in the grain, bestowing it lavishly upon the starving. Spirit revives this small vine, and I crush its bunches of grapes and pour out the juice for the thirsty. The sky fills this lamp with oil, and I light it and place it in the window of my house for those who pass by in the black of night. I do these things because I live thereby, and when the days prevent me from doing so and the nights shackle my hand, I shall seek death. For death most resembles a prophet who is without honor in his own land or a poet who is a stranger among his people.

Human beings clamor like a tempest while I sigh in silence, for I have found that the violence of the storm subsides and the abyss of time swallows it, whereas a sigh endures as long as God.

Human beings cling to matter that is cold as snow whereas I seek the flame of love so that I might place it in my breast, where it will devour my ribs and destroy my insides. For I have discovered that matter kills painlessly, but love revives us through torments.

Human beings separate into factions and tribes and adhere to countries and regions whereas I see my essence as foreign to any one land and alien to any single people. The entire earth is my homeland and the human family is my clan. For I have found human beings to be weak, and it is small-minded for them to divide themselves up; the earth is cramped, so that only ignorance leads people to partition it into realms and principalities.

Human beings unite in destroying the temples of the spirit and cooperate in building the edifices of the body. I alone celebrate in elegies. For I listen and hear from within me a voice of hope saying, 'Just as love restores life to the human heart through pain, so foolishness teaches the paths to knowledge. Pain and foolishness lead to great bliss and complete knowledge, for Eternal Wisdom created nothing under the sun in vain.'

II

I crave my homeland for its beauty and love its inhabitants for their poverty. Yet when my people set out to defend what they call nationalism and march upon the homeland of my neighbors – plundering their wealth, killing their men, making orphans of their children, and widows of their women, spilling the blood of their sons on the earth, and feeding the flesh of their youths to beasts of prey – then I hate my country and its inhabitants.

I rhapsodize, remembering my birthplace, and I long for the house in which I was raised. But when a vagrant passes by and asks for shelter in that house and for food from its residents, and when he is refused and cast out, then my rhapsodies become dirges and my yearning turns to disregard. Then I say in my essence, 'The house that is too miserly to share bread with the needy or bedding with one who asks for it is most deserving of all houses to be torn down and destroyed.'

I love my birthplace with some of the same love I shower upon my region; I love my region with a part of the love I bestow on my homeland; and I love the whole earth, because it is the place where humanity thrives, and sacred humanity is the spirit of divinity in this world. This humanity stands among ruins, hiding its naked form with tattered rags, shedding hot tears on its withered cheeks, calling its children with a voice that fills the ether with howling and lamentation, while its children are too busy with their anthems of group loyalty to hear its call and too concerned with burnishing their swords to heed its tears. This humanity is seated alone, imploring its people, who do not hear. Or, if one hears, he comes near and wipes away its tears and consoles it in its afflictions. And the people say, 'Leave it alone, for tears affect only the weak.'

Humanity is the spirit of divinity on earth. That divinity which walks among the nations and speaks of love, pointing toward the paths of life, while the people laugh and mock its words and teachings. That divinity which the Nazarene heard yesterday (and they crucified him), which Socrates perceived (and they poisoned him), and which today the followers of the Nazarene and of Socrates have heard. They say its name aloud before the people, and the people cannot kill them. But they ridicule them instead, saying, 'Ridicule is crueler than killing, and more bitter.'

Jerusalem proved unable to kill the Nazarene, for he is alive forever; nor could Athens execute Socrates, for he is immortal. Nor shall derision prove powerful against those who listen to humanity or those who follow in the footsteps of divinity, for they shall live forever. Forever.

III

You are my brother, and both of us are sons of a single, universal, and sacred spirit. You are my likeness, for we are prisoners of the same body, fashioned from the same clay. You are my companion on the byways of life, my helper in perceiving the essence of reality concealed behind the mists. You are a human being and I have loved you, my brother.

Say about me what you will, for tomorrow will pass judgment on you and your words will be clear testimony in its court and pertinent evidence before its justice.

Take from me what you will, for you only pilfer wealth, a portion of which belongs to you, and property that I monopolize because of my desires. You deserve some of it, should it please you.

Do with me what you will, for you are unable to touch my reality. Spill my blood and burn my body, but my soul will never feel the pain and you will never kill it. Fetter my hands and legs with chains and cast me into an unlit stockade, for you will never succeed in imprisoning my thoughts, which are free as a gale that lists in the sky without limit or boundary.

You are my brother, and I love you.

I love you when you bow in your mosque, kneel in your temple, pray in your church. For you and I are sons of one religion, and it is the spirit. The leaders of the branches of this religion are like fingers of the hand of divinity, which point to the perfection of the soul.

I love you for the sake of your reality, which emanates

from the Universal Intellect; that reality which I cannot see now because of my blindness but which I consider holy because it is among the works of the soul; that reality that will encounter my own reality in the next world, where they will mingle like the aromas of flowers and become a single universal reality, eternal because love and beauty are never-ending.

I love you because I have seen you weak before the heartless and powerful, poor and needy before the lofty mansions of the grasping rich. For this reason I wept for your sake, and through my tears I saw you in the arms of justice, who smiles at you and heaps scorn on your persecutors. You are my brother, and I love you.

I V

You are my brother, and I love you. Why then do you dispute with me?

Why do you come to my country and try to subdue me, in order to please leaders who seek glory by exploiting your words and happiness by appropriating the fruits of your labors? Why do you forsake your wife and little ones, following death to a remote land for the sake of commanders who wish to buy high rank with your blood and great honor with the grief of your parents? But is it high honor for a human being to make war on his brother? Let us raise up, then, a statue to Cain and sing out the praises of Annas.

They say, O my brother, that self-protection is a basic natural principle. But I have seen those ambitious for prestige attempt to instill in you a love of self-sacrifice, in order to make slaves of your brothers. They say that the desire to survive requires an attack on the rights of others. And I say, 'Safeguarding the rights of others is the most noble and beautiful end of a human being.' But I say, as well, 'If my survival caused another to perish, then death would be sweeter and more beloved. And if I discovered that the one who was about to kill me was not noble, loving, and pure, I would relish offering up my life by my own hand to eternity, before my time came.'

Egotism, my brother, was the origin of blind competition, and competition generated group loyalty, and group loyalty founded political power, which in turn became a motive for strife and enslavement. The soul asserts the rule of wisdom and justice over ignorance and tyranny, and it rejects the authority that extracts from mines knives and blades with which to spread folly and oppression. This is the political power that devastated Babylon, razed Jerusalem to its foundations, and pulled down Rome's edifices. It is they who inaugurated bloodshed and killing, as a result of which the people laud them as great, and the chroniclers glorify their names, and books do not refuse to preserve their battles deep inside themselves, just as the earth does not refuse to carry them on its back, even while they dye its face red with pure blood . . . What has impelled you, O my brother, to surrender to your tempter, and has caused you to be devoted to the one who harms you? True power is the wisdom that protects the universal, just, natural law. Where is the justice of political power if it executes the murderer and jails the plunderer, and then itself marches upon neighboring lands, killing thousands and pillaging the very hills? What do the nationalists say about killers punishing murderers and thieves sentencing looters?

You are my brother, and I love you, and love is justice in the most sublime of its manifestations. If I were not equitable in my love for you in every country, I would be a charlatan, concealing the ugliness of egotism in the splendid finery of love.

BEAUTY

Beauty is the religion
of the sages.
An Indian Poet

You who roamed distracted in the byways of proliferous religions and roved the valleys of contrary doctrines; you who found the freedom to disbelieve preferable to the chains of submission and the arenas of denial safer than the redoubts of obedience; you adopted beauty as your religion and revered it as your lord. For it is manifest in the perfection of the creatures and is apparent in the conclusions reached by the intellect. Cast aside those who liken godliness to whimsy and who try to combine their greed for wealth with their desire for a happy afterlife. Believe in the divinity of beauty, which is the beginning of your appreciation of life and the origin of your love for joy. Then turn in repentance unto it, for it draws your hearts nigh to the throne of woman, who is the mirror of your feelings; and it is the trainer of your souls in the realm of nature, which is where your lives originated.

You who are lost in the night of idle talk and drowned in the abyss of false imaginings, know that in beauty is a reality that extinguishes doubt and prevents skepticism, a dazzling light that safeguards you from the gloom of falsehood.

Contemplate the wakefulness of spring and the advent of the morn, for beauty is the lot of those who contemplate.

Listen to the melodies of the birds, the rustling of the boughs, the purling of the stream; beauty is the share of listeners. Observe the meekness of the child, the gracefulness of the youth, the power of the mature, and the wisdom of the aged; beauty is the charm of those who watch.

Rhapsodize about the narcissus of the eyes, the rose of the cheeks, the anemones of the lips; beauty is glorified by those who rhapsodize. Praise the tree-limb stature, the night-black hair, the ivory neck; beauty is gladdened by those who praise. Hallow the body as a temple to comeliness and sanctify the heart as a sacrifice to love; love recompenses the adorers.

Sing praises, you to whom the verses of beauty have been revealed, and rejoice; for no fear comes upon you, nor do you sorrow.

CHILDREN OF GODS,
SCIONS OF APES

How amazing time is, and how amazing we are. Time has been transformed, and we have changed; it has advanced and set us in motion; it has unveiled its face, inspiring us with bewilderment and exhilaration.

Yesterday we complained of time and feared it, but today we love and embrace it. Indeed, we have begun to perceive its purposes and characteristics, and to comprehend its secrets and enigmas.

Yesterday we crawled apprehensively, like phantoms quaking between the terrors of night and the horrors of day. Today we stride zealously toward the summits of mountains, where raging storms ensconce themselves and blazing lightning and crashing thunder are engendered.

Yesterday we ate bread kneaded with blood and drank water mingled with tears. But today we dine on manna from the hands of dawn-sprites and sip wine fragrant with the breaths of spring.

Yesterday we were playthings in the hand of fate, and fate was a drunken tyrant, bending us to the right and then to the left. But today fate has sobered up, and we play with it and it plays back; we jest with it and it laughs; then we lead it and it follows behind us.

Yesterday we burned incense before graven images and immolated sacrifices before irascible gods. But today we light incense only for ourselves and offer sacrifices only to our own essences. For the greatest and most gloriously beautiful of deities has made his temple in our breasts.

Yesterday we obeyed kings and bent our necks before emperors. But today we kneel only to the truth, follow only beauty, and obey only love.

Yesterday we humbly lowered our eyes before priests and dreaded the visions of oracles. But today the times have changed and we have changed, and we stare only at the countenance of the sun, listen only to the melodies of the sea, and tremble only with the typhoon.

Yesterday we demolished the thrones of our souls in order to build from them the tombs of our grandfathers. But today our souls have been transformed into holy altars, which the ghosts of dusty centuries cannot approach and the grizzled fingers of the dead cannot touch.

We were a silent, hidden thought in the folds of oblivion, and we have become a voice that causes the heavens to tremble.

We were a faint spark buried in ash, but have become a fire blazing above the sheltered ravine.

How many are the nights that we stayed up late, cradling our heads on the dirt with snow for a blanket, weeping for lost friendships and possessions. How many are the days we spent lying about like sheep without a shepherd, nibbling at our thoughts and chewing our emotions, remaining hungry and thirsty. How often we stood between waning day and onrushing night, mourning our fading youth, yearning for an unknown person, lonely for some obscure reason, staring at a dark, empty sky, listening to the groans of silence and nothingness.

Those centuries passed, like a thieving wolf-pack through a cemetery, but today the sky has awakened and we have awakened. We spend white nights on celestial beds, staying up late with our imaginations, keeping our thoughts company and embracing our passions. Flames glimmer all around us, and we seize them with steady fingers; the spirits of genies ascend all around us, and we address them unequivocally. Hosts of the angels pass by us, and we entice them by the yearning in our hearts and make them drunk with the rhapsodies of our spirits.

Yesterday we were and today we have become, and this is the will of the gods for their children. What, then, is your will, scions of the apes?

Have you advanced even one stride forward since you issued from fissures in the earth? Or have you lifted your gaze toward the heights since the demons opened your eyes? Have you pronounced a single word from the Book of Truth since the serpents kissed your mouths with theirs?

Or have you listened even an instant to the song of life since death stopped up your ears?

I have been passing by you for 70,000 years, and have seen you metamorphose like insects in the corners of grottoes. Seven minutes ago I looked at you from behind the pane of my window and found you ambling in filthy alleyways, led by the devils of apathy, the chains of servitude shackling your feet and the wings of death fluttering above your heads. You are today as you were yesterday and shall remain tomorrow and thereafter, just as I saw you in the beginning.

Yesterday we were and today we have become, for this is the wont of the gods with the children of gods. What, then, is the way of apes with you, O scions of the apes?

HAVE MERCY,
MY SOUL

How long will you lament, my soul, when you know how frail I am? How long will you clamor, when I possess only human words with which to depict your dreams?

Look, my soul, for I have spent my life listening to your teachings. Think, my torturer, for I have worn out my body following your footsteps.

My heart was my monarch, but now it has become your slave. My patience was my confidante, but under your influence it has become my critic. Youth was my boon companion, but now it reproaches me. And all this has befallen me from the gods. How will you demand more, and what do you crave?

I have repudiated my essence and abandoned the delights of my life. I forsook my glory, and only you remain to me, so judge with justice, for justice is your glory. Or summon death and release your ward from prison.

Have mercy, my soul. For you have burdened me with a love that I cannot bear: you and love are a unified force, whereas I and matter are fragmented in our weakness, and can your bonds long persist when stretched between force and weakness?

Have mercy, my soul. For you showed me happiness from a great distance. You and happiness are on a lofty mountain, while wretchedness and I subsist in the depths of a ravine. Can loftiness and abasement ever meet?

Have mercy, my soul. For you revealed love to me and then concealed it. You and your beauty in light, and ignorance and I in the darkness. Can light and darkness ever mix?

You, my soul, rejoice in the afterlife before it even arrives, while this body suffers from life even while it lives.

You approach eternity in haste, and this body takes slow steps toward annihilation. You do not tarry and it does not hasten; and this, my soul, is the utmost misery.

You rise toward the heights, attracted by the heavens, whereas this body plummets downward because of the earth's gravity. You do not console it, and it does not congratulate you; and that is rancor.

You, my soul, are rich with your wisdom, but this body is poor by reason of its instincts. You show it no forbearance, and it does not follow; and that is the utmost wretchedness.

You go in the silence of the night toward the beloved and enjoy his embraces, and this body remains ever a martyr to yearning and separation.

Have mercy, my soul; have mercy.

MY SOUL IS HEAVY LADEN
WITH ITS FRUITS

My soul is heavy laden with its fruits, so is there anyone hungering who will harvest them, and eat of them, and be satiated?

Is there no one among the people who has been fasting who will graciously break the fast upon my offspring and relieve me of the burden of my fecundity and abundance?

My soul is collapsing beneath the weight of gold ore and silver. Will anyone among the people fill his pockets and lighten my load?

My soul is overflowing with the wine of eons. Is there anyone thirsting who will pour, and drink, and slake his thirst?

There stands a man in the middle of the road, thrusting toward passers-by a handful of gems, calling to them: 'Look! Have mercy and snatch them from me. Take pity and relieve me of what I have!' As for the people, they walked on, paying no attention.

Indeed, would that he were a beggar, entreating and stretching out his quivering hand toward the pedestrians, and bringing it back, empty and trembling. Would that he were sitting there blind, and the people were passing by, indifferent.

There is the wealthy, munificent sheik, who raises his tent between the white, unexplored peaks and the foothills of the mountains. He lights the fire of a hospitable reception every night and sends his servants to monitor the roads, in hopes that they will lead to him a guest whom he might feed and honor. But the trails prove miserly, yielding no caller who might eat of his free banquet and sending no seeker to accept his gifts.

Would that he were a cast-out pauper!

Would that he were a homeless vagabond who roamed the lands, a staff in his hand and a begging bowl at his waist, and that when evening came the bends in the alleyways gathered together him and his companions among the vagrants and tramps, and that he sat next to them and shared out the bread of charity.

There is the daughter of the great king, who awakens from her repose and rises from her bed. She clothes herself in purple and lavender, adorns herself with pearls and sapphires, sprays perfume on her hair, and soaks her fingers in liquid ambergris. Then she walks in her garden, where droplets of dew moisten the hems of her robes.

In the quiet of the night the daughter of the great king walks in her garden, looking for her beloved, but no one in all the realm of her father loves her.

Would that she were the daughter of a peasant, herding her father's sheep in the valleys and returning at night to his hovel, her feet dusty with her toil, the odor of vineyards lingering in the folds of her clothing. Then, when night descended and the people of the quarter had fallen asleep, she would steal away to the place where her lover was awaiting.

Would that she were a nun in a convent, her heart burning with incense, the fragrance of which the wind would waft abroad. Her spirit would ignite a candle, and the ether would convey the light of her soul. She would genuflect in prayer, and the specters of the unseen would bear her prayers to the treasure-hold of time, where the devotions of worshipers are safeguarded beside the flames of lovers and the misgivings of hermits.

Would that she were aged and timeworn, sitting and sunning herself with the one who shared her youth. For that would be better than to be the daughter of the great king whose realm contains no suitor to eat of her heart like bread or drink of her blood like wine.

My soul is heavy laden with its fruits; is there anyone on earth hungering who will harvest them, and eat them, and be satiated?

My soul is overflowing with its wine. Is there anyone thirsting who will pour, and drink, and slake his thirst?

Would that I were a never-blossoming tree, which gave no fruit. For the pain of fecundity is more bitter than the anguish of barrenness, and the torments of the well-to-do with their inalienable wealth hold horrors greater than any suffered by a pauper who goes without food.

Would that I were a dry well, and that the people tossed

stones into me, for that would be easier than to be a spring of flowing water that the thirsty pass by, and from which they avoid drinking.

Would that I were a crushed cane, trampled beneath the feet, for that would be better than to be a lyre with silver strings in the house of a master who has lost all his fingers and whose family is deaf.

THE VISIT OF
WISDOM

In the quiet of the night Wisdom came and stood beside my bed, gazing at me like a doting mother. She wiped away my tears and said, 'I heard the cry of your soul and came to solace you. Open your heart to me, that I might fill it with light. Ask me, and I shall show you the path of truth.'

I said, 'Who am I, O Wisdom, and how did I arrive in this ghastly place? What are these powerful longings, numerous books, and eldritch markings? What are these thoughts that pass like a flock of doves? What is this speech, ordered in affection and scattered in delight? What are these consequences that sadden and enrapture, that embrace my spirit and besiege my heart? What are these eyes fixed upon me, that gaze upon my innermost self and ignore my pain? What are these voices mourning over my days, singing of my childhood? What is this youth, who plays with my desires, mocks my sentiments, forgets the deeds of yesterday, rejoices in the trivialities of the moment, and loathes the tardiness of tomorrow? What is this world that is hastening me toward I know not what, viewing me with contempt? What is this earth, its mouth gaping to swallow bodies, whose bosom offers relief to the abode of ambition? What is this person who acquiesces in loving happiness, but accepts hell if he cannot attain it; who seeks the kiss of life and receives the blows of death; who buys a moment of pleasure with a year of regrets; who surrenders to the slumber and dreams that call to him; who walks along the canals of ignorance to the gulf of darkness? What are all these things, O Wisdom?'

She said, 'You desire, O mortal, to view this world through the eyes of a god, and wish to comprehend the mysteries of the world to come by means of your human intellect; and this is the utmost folly. Go out into the open country, and you will find the bee hovering over flowers and the eagle picking apart its prey. Enter the house of your neighbor, and you will see a child bedazzled by the fire's rays, while the mother busies herself with housework. Imitate the bee and do not spend the days of spring gazing upon the deeds of the eagle. Be as the child and delight in the flame's brightness, and pay no heed to your mother and her affairs.

'All that you see was and is for your sake. The numerous books, uncanny markings, and beautiful thoughts are the ghosts of souls who preceded you. The speech they weave is a link between you and your human siblings. The consequences that cause sorrow and rapture are the seeds that the past has sown in the field of the soul, and by which the future shall profit . . . This youth who plays with your desires is the very same person who opened the door of your heart so as to flood it with light. This earth with its gaping maw is the one who delivers you from bondage to your body. This world that hastens you is your heart, and your heart is all that you conceive of as a world. The person you consider ignorant and insignificant is the one who came from God, that he might learn bliss from grief and knowledge from gloom.'

Wisdom placed her hand on my feverish forehead and said, 'Advance and never halt, for advancing is perfection. Advance and do not fear the thorns in the path, for they draw only corrupt blood.'

THE POET OF BAALBEK

IN THE CITY OF BAALBEK, 112 B.C.

The king seated himself upon his gilded throne, which was encircled by blazing lamps and ignited thuribles. The generals and priests sat to his right and his left, and the troops and slaves stood before him like graven idols before the sun's countenance.

The chanters finished their anthems, and their breaths vanished into the folds of night's robes, while the grand vizier stood before the king and said, in a voice tremulous with feeble old age, 'O great king, a sage of India arrived in the city yesterday, exhibiting strange states and teaching many doctrines, the likes of which we have never heard. He calls upon the people to believe that spirits clothe themselves first in one body, then in another, so that souls transmigrate from century to century until they attain perfection, entering the ranks of the gods. He has come tonight, requesting an audience with you, so that he might lay out his teachings before you.'

The king nodded, smiling, and said, 'From the land of India come wonders and marvels. So summon him that we may listen to his proof.'

A minute had not elapsed before there entered the hall a middle-aged man with a brown complexion, an awe-inspiring visage, large eyes, and wide features, which spoke without words of profound mysteries and occult yearnings. After he bowed, seeking permission to speak, he raised his head, eyes gleaming, and began to discourse on his heresy. He delineated the way in which spirits move from one bodily temple to another, advancing by the means that they choose, progressing through the influence of the things they experience, swayed by the distinguished persons who elevate and strengthen them, growing by the love that brings them gladness and misery . . . Then he turned to the manner in which souls migrate from place to place, searching for the perfections they require, repenting in their present of the sins they committed in their past, reaping in one realm what they sowed in another.

When he had spoken at length, and the signs of boredom and displeasure had appeared in the king's features, the grand vizier drew nigh to the sage and whispered in his ear, 'That will suffice for now; leave the discussion to another opportunity.'

The yogi withdrew and seated himself among the priests, his lids closed as though his eyes were exhausted from gazing at the enigmas and mysteries of being.

After a silence like a prophetic trance, the king turned to his right, then to his left, then asked, 'Where is our poet? Some time has passed since we have seen him. What has happened to him? He used to attend our gatherings every evening.'

One of the priests said, 'I saw him a week ago, sitting in the courtyard of the temple of Astarte, staring with a fixed and woeful gaze toward the distant twilight, as though he had lost an ode among the clouds.'

One of the generals said, 'I saw him yesterday standing among the cypress and willow trees. I hailed him, but he did not return my greeting, remaining drowned in the sea of his thoughts and dreams.'

The chief of the eunuchs said, 'I saw him today in the garden of the palace. I approached him and found his complexion sallow and his face wan, his tears flirting with his eyelids and his miseries toying with his breath.'

The king said, in a voice filled with apprehension, 'Go and look for him, and bring him to us posthaste, for his condition has caused us anxiety.'

The slaves and foot soldiers departed, seeking out the poet, and the king and his courtiers remained silent, bewildered and expectant, as though their souls had sensed the presence of an invisible phantasm standing in the middle of the hall.

After a time, the chief of the eunuchs returned and collapsed at the feet of the king, like a bird transfixed by a hunter's arrow. The king screamed at him, 'What news? What happened?'

The black man raised his head and said, quivering, 'We found the poet dead in the garden of the palace.'

The king stood up, his mien one of grief and sorrow. Then he left for the garden, preceded by the lamp-bearers and followed by the generals and priests. When they reached the environs of the garden, where the almond trees and pomegranate shrubs stood, the yellow rays of the lamps revealed to them a lifeless cadaver thrown upon the grass like the stalk of a withered rose.

One of the courtiers said, 'Look how he embraces his lyre, as though it were a beautiful girl whom he loved and who loved him, with whom he made a suicide pact.'

One of the generals said, 'He is still staring off into the depths of the sky, as was his habit, as though he sees among the planets the image of an unknown god.'

The chief of the priests turned to the king: 'Tomorrow we shall bury him in the shadow of the holy temple of Astarte, and the people of the city shall walk behind his bier while young men recite his odes and virgins scatter flowers over his tomb. He was a great poet, so let the burial ceremonies be great.'

The king shook his head without lifting his eyes from the face of the poet, arrayed in the veil of death, then said slowly, 'No, no. We ignored him while he was alive, filling the far corners of the realm with the apparitions of his soul and perfuming the sky with his breaths. Were we now to honor him in death, the gods would mock us and the brides of the spirits in the meadows and valleys would laugh at us. Bury him here where he gave up his spirit, and leave the lyre in his arms. If any of you wishes to honor him, go to his house and inform his sons that the king neglected his poet, who died, sorrowful, alone, solitary.'

Then he looked around him and added, 'Where is the Indian philosopher?'

The philosopher stepped forward and said, 'I am here, mighty king.'

The king said, 'Speak. Speak, O sage. Will the laws of the universe return me as a king to this world, and return him as a poet? Will they clad my spirit in the body of the son of a mighty ruler, and incarnate his soul in the body of a matchless poet? Will the fates summon him once more before the face of eternity, to make poetry of life, and reinstate me so that I may bestow blessings on him and gladden his heart with gifts and presents?'

The philosopher replied, 'All that spirits desire, spirits attain. The same cosmic law that brings back the delights of spring when winter ends will restore you as a mighty king and him as a great poet.'

The king's features relaxed and his soul was reanimated. He walked toward the palace, thinking about the words of the Indian sage, repeating to himself, 'All that spirits desire, spirits attain.'

II
IN CAIRO, EGYPT, 1912 A.D.

The moon rose and cast its silver sash over the city, and the khedive sat on the balcony of his palace, surveying the clear sky. He mused upon where the centuries that had passed, one after the other, over the banks of the Nile had led; he sought to understand the deeds of the monarchs and conquerors who had stood before the awesome Sphinx, reviewing in his imagination the procession of peoples and societies that time had caused to march from the environs of the pyramids to Abdeen Palace.

When the scope of his thoughts widened and the stage of his daydreams broadened, he turned to his boon companion, sitting nearby, and said, 'Tonight our soul has an inclination toward poetry. Recite some.'

The king's intimate nodded his head and began reciting an ode by a pre-Islamic poet. The khedive cut him off, saying, 'Recite something from a more recent time.'

The boon companion nodded again, and began to read a poem by a contemporary of the Prophet.

The khedive interrupted him again. 'Something more modern, more modern.'

For a third time the royal intimate nodded and chanted some Andalusian stanzas.

The khedive said, 'Recite an ode by a contemporary author.'

The boon companion put his hand to his forehead as though

wishing to remember all the verses penned by the poets of that age. Abruptly, his eyes flashed and his face cheered. He began to recite imaginative verse which possessed a magical resonance, exquisite, original figures of speech, and subtle, rare allusions that drew near to the soul and filled it with rays of light, encompassing the heart and melting it with affection.

The khedive stared at his companion, enraptured by the melody and the conceits of the verses. He sensed the presence of invisible hands luring him away from that place to a distant spot. He asked, 'Who wrote those verses?'

His confidant replied, 'The poet of Baalbek.'

The poet of Baalbek! The strange words reverberated in the khedive's ears, giving rise within his noble spirit to the ghosts of desires deceptive in their clarity and powerful in their delicacy.

The poet of Baalbek, both an ancient and a modern name, recalled to the king's mind the traces of forgotten days, awakened in the depths of his breast slumbering memories and imaginings, and delineated before his eyes – in strokes like traces of mist – the image of a dead young man embracing a lyre, around whom stood generals and priests and ministers.

That vision faded from before the khedive's eyes, as a dream flees before the advent of morn, and he stood and walked, arms crossed. He repeated again and again the verse of the Arabian Prophet: 'You were dead, and He revived you; then He will cause you to die, and He will revive you; then unto Him shall ye return.'

He turned to his companion, saying, 'We are pleased at

the presence of the poet from Baalbek in our realm, and we shall draw him near and bestow honors upon him.' After a moment he added in a subdued voice, 'A poet is a bird of unearthly excellence, who escapes from his celestial realm and arrives in this world warbling. If we do not cherish him, he spreads his wings and flies back to his homeland.'

Night dissipated, and the heavens slipped out of their star-sequined robes, donning a chemise woven from the rays of morning. And the soul of the king of the land staggered between the wonders of existence and the riddles of life.

BETWEEN REALITY
AND FANTASY

Life has borne us from place to place, and the fates convey us from one spot to another, but we see only the obstacles that stand in our way and hear only the voice that terrifies us.

Beauty manifests itself to us on the throne of its splendor, and we draw near to it; in the name of yearning we defile its hem and pull off its diadem of purity. Love passes by us cloaked in a robe of kindness, but we fear it and conceal ourselves in the grottoes of darkness; or we follow it and commit outrages in its name. The wise among us construe it as a heavy yoke, but it is more delicate than the breaths of flowers and more subtle than the breezes of Lebanon. Wisdom stands at the turn in the road and calls upon us publicly, but we consider it false and despise its adherents. Liberty summons us to its table, that we might savor its wine and fare; so we go and make gluttons of ourselves, transforming that table into a stage for vulgarity and a scene of self-abasement. Nature extends to us the hand of loyalty, asking from us that we delight in its comeliness; but we fear its quietude and take refuge in the city, where we crowd in upon one another like a flock of sheep that spies a hungry wolf. Truth visits us, led by the smile of a child or the kiss of a beloved, but we slam the door of our emotions, excluding it and abandoning it like a vile criminal. The human heart appeals to us for help and the soul calls out to us, but we are more deaf than a stone, unable to comprehend or understand. And when anyone listens to the cry of his heart and the call of his soul, we say, 'That one is possessed,' and we wash our hands of him.

Thus pass the nights, while we remain heedless. The days greet us, but we are frightened of both days and nights. We draw near to the earth, and gods join our company; we pass by the bread of life, and famine feasts on our faculties. How beloved life is to us, and how remote we are from life.

A HANDFUL OF SAND
ON THE SHORE

The grief that comes with love sings, the grief that comes with knowledge speaks, the grief that comes with desire whispers, and the grief that comes with poverty laments. But there is a grief more profound than love, nobler than knowledge, stronger than desire, and more bitter than want. It, however, is mute, lacking any voice, though its eyes scintillate like the stars.

When you complain of a misfortune to your neighbors, you bestow on them a piece of your heart. If they are kind-hearted, they thank you. But if they are small-minded, they despise you.

Progress lies not in enhancing what is, but in advancing toward what will be.

Poverty is a veil that obscures the face of greatness. An appeal is a mask covering the face of tribulation.

When a savage feels hunger, he picks a piece of fruit from a tree and eats it; when a civilized man feels hunger, he buys a piece of fruit from a vendor, who has bought it from someone who bought it from someone who bought it from someone who picked it from a tree.

Art is a step from what is obvious and well-known toward what is arcane and concealed.

Some people encourage me to trust them, so that they may enjoy the delights of my forbearance.

I have never perceived the inside of a man who did not consider me indebted to him.

The earth takes a breath and we are born, then exhales it and we die.

The eye of a human being is a microscope, which makes the world seem bigger than it really is.

I wash my hands of a people who consider impudence to be courage and tenderness to be cowardice.

I wash my hands of those who imagine chattering to be knowledge, silence to be ignorance, and affection to be art.

It might be that for us to consider a matter difficult constitutes the easiest path toward it.

They say to me: 'Should you see a person sleeping, do not wake him, for he might be dreaming of his liberty.' I say to them: 'Were I to see a person sleeping, I would awaken him and speak with him about liberty.'

Contradiction is the lowest level of intelligence.

Beauty captivates us, but the greatest beauty sets us free even from its own essence.

Zeal is a volcano, on the peak of which the grass of indecisiveness does not grow.

The river strives earnestly to reach the sea, whether the mill's waterwheel gets broken or not.

The author creates from thought and emotion, and clothes them in words. The researcher creates from words to which he adds a little thought and emotion.

You eat quickly but walk slowly; have you not then eaten with your legs and walked upon your palms?

Whenever you experience great joy or sorrow, the world is diminished in your eyes.

Knowledge cultivates your seeds and does not sow in you seeds.

I have never hated anyone except when I fashioned a weapon from my rancor in self-defense. Yet were I not weak, I would not have adopted that sort of weapon.

If the grandfather of the grandfather of Jesus had known what was hidden within him, he would have stood humble and awe-struck before his soul.

Love is a happiness that trembles.

They consider me to have sharp and penetrating vision because I see them through the mesh of a sieve.

I never felt the pain of loneliness until the people praised my chattering faults and condemned my mute virtues.

Among the people are murderers who have never shed blood, thieves who have never stolen anything, and liars who have never spoken anything but the truth.

The reality that requires a proof is only half a reality.

Lo, keep me away from a wisdom that does not weep, a philosophy that does not laugh, and a grandeur that will not bow its head before children.

O Rational Existence, who is veiled by the outward appearances of beings and is present in beings, of beings, and for beings, you hear me because you are my present and my essence. And you see me because you are the vision of all living things. Sow in my spirit a seed from your wisdom, that it may grow as a fresh shoot in your forest and bear one of your fruits. Amen.

MY FRIEND

Did you but know, my destitute friend, that the poverty that sentences you to wretchedness is precisely what inspires you with a knowledge of justice and allows you to perceive the essence of life, then you would be content with the destiny ordained by God. I said 'knowledge of justice' because the attention of the wealthy is diverted by their treasures from this knowledge. And I said, 'the essence of life' because the powerful are distracted therefrom by their pursuit of glory. Rejoice, then, in justice because you are its tongue, and in life, because you are its book. Be glad, for you are the source of virtue for your benefactors and the bestower of virtue on those who take your hand.

If you but comprehended, my forlorn comrade, that the burdens that have defeated you are the same power that illumines your heart and elevates your soul from the plane of ridicule to the station of esteem, then you would be content therewith as your inheritance and would accept its effects as your mentor. You would know that life is a chain with links, some intertwined with others, and that grief is a golden link that divides acquiescence in the outcomes of the present from enjoyment of the delights of the future, just as morning divides sleep from waking.

My friend, poverty manifests the nobility of the soul, and opulence brings out its blameworthy tendencies. Sadness lends delicacy to the emotions, whereas joy sullies them. For human beings still employ riches and joy as means to excess, just as they commit evil in the name of the Book that forbids it, and do in the name of humanity what humanity disavows.

Were poverty to be wiped out and sorrow to vanish, the soul would become a blank scroll save for characters that signify egotism and a love of aggrandizement and words that connote earthly appetites. For I looked, and found divinity, the spiritual essence in human beings that cannot be bought with lucre nor augmented by the pleasures of libertines. I contemplated and saw the affluent forsaking their divinity and safeguarding their wealth, and the slaves of the age abandoning their divine selves to follow their pleasures.

The hour that you spend, you the destitute, with your wife and little ones after you come from the fields is a symbol of the human family of the future, a token of the happiness of coming generations. The life that the rich pass among their assets is a contemptible life that recalls the burrowing of the worm in graves; it is a symbol of fear.

The tears that you spill, you the sorrowful, are sweeter than the laughter of snobs and the guffaws of scoffers. Those tears cleanse the heart from the filth of rancor and teach the one who sheds them how the broken-hearted share his feelings; they are the tears of the Nazarene.

The power that you sowed, you the poor, which the rich and powerful have exploited, will return to you. For the law of nature is that things return to their source. The tribulation you have endured, you the grief-stricken, will be transformed into bliss by the edict of heaven.

Coming generations will learn equality from poverty, and love from woes.

THE PHILOSOPHY
OF LOGIC
(Or, Knowledge of the Self)

One rainy night in Beirut, Salim Effendi Duaybis sat before his desk, on which lay heaps of old books and scattered papers. He turned the pages, raising his head from time to time to release a cloud of tobacco smoke from his thick lips. He held in his hands a philosophical treatise that Socrates had revealed to his disciple Plato, on 'Knowing the Self.'

Salim Effendi pondered the lines of that precious treatise, calling to mind what the philosophers and sages had said about it, so that his thoughts encompassed every stray thought of every Western thinker and his memory extended to every saying thereon of an Eastern teacher. When his self began to drown in the subject of knowledge of the self, he rose suddenly and raised his arms, shouting in his loudest voice, 'Yes, yes, knowledge of the self is the mother of all knowledge. So it is incumbent on me to know my self, to know it completely, to know its minutiae, its characteristics, its subtleties, and its very atoms. I must unveil the mysteries of my self, and efface all confusion from my heart's hidden corners. Indeed, I must elucidate the meaning of my spiritual being to my material being, and the secrets of my material existence to my spiritual existence.'

He said all that with an odd enthusiasm, while in his eyes the flame of 'the love of knowledge' – knowledge of the soul – was ignited. He went into a neighboring room and stood like a statue before a great mirror that extended from the floor to the ceiling, staring at his reflection, scrutinizing his face, contemplating the shape of his head, the lines of his build, and his general appearance.

He remained standing, immobile, in that state for half an hour, as though Eternal Thought had revealed to him ideas terrifying in their sublimity, through which he had uncovered the innermost recesses of his spirit and filled the emptiness of his self with light. Then he quietly opened his mouth and said to himself:

'I am short of stature, but so were Napoleon and Victor Hugo.

'I have a low forehead, but so did Socrates and Spinoza.

'I am bald, but so was Shakespeare.

'My nose is big and inclines to one side, like that of Savanarola, Voltaire, and George Washington.

'My eyes are weak, as were those of the Apostle Paul and Nietzsche.

'My mouth is thick and my bottom lip protrudes, like those of Cicero and Louis XIV.

'My neck is thick, but that was true of Hannibal and Marcus Antonius.

'My ears are long and stick out inelegantly, like those of Bruno and Cervantes.

'My cheekbones are prominent and my cheeks sunken, just as were those of Lafayette and Lincoln.

'I have a receding chin, like Goldsmith and William Pitt.

'My shoulders are mismatched, one higher than the other, like Gambetta and Adib Ishaq.

'My hands have thick palms and short fingers, like Blake and Danton.

'In sum, my body is weak and feeble, as is the wont of thinkers who tire their bodies in seeking their selves. The strange thing is that I cannot sit and write or study without a pot of coffee at my side, and Balzac was the same way. In addition, I have an inclination to associate with the rabble and the simple folk, just as did Tolstoy and Maxim Gorky. A day or two can pass without my washing my face or hands, and in that I resemble Beethoven and Walt Whitman. Amazingly enough, I am comfortable listening to news of women and what they do in the absence of their husbands, like Boccaccio and Rabelais. As for my thirst for wine, it rivals that of Noah, Abu Nuwas, De Musset, and Marlowe. My appetite for fine cuisine and smorgasbords compares with the voracity of Peter the Great and Emir Bashir al-Shihabi.'

Salim Effendi ceased talking to himself for a moment and put his fingertips to his brow. He added, 'There I am. This is my reality. I am a collection of the attributes possessed by the greatest men from the beginning of history to our own day, and a youth who encompasses all these traits must be responsible for some magnificent achievement in this world.

'The beginning of wisdom is knowledge of the self. I have known myself tonight, and on this night I shall initiate the great work with which I have been charged by the Idea of this world, which has placed deep within me divers and contradictory elements. I have been closely associated with great men, from Noah to Socrates, from Boccaccio to Ahmad Faris al-Shidyaq. I know not what great work I shall undertake. But a man who combines in his person matter with spiritual essence, as I do, such a man is one of the miracles of the days and one of the prodigies of the nights . . . I have known my self and, yes, even the gods have known my self. Let my soul live and my essence subsist, let existence remain in being until my goal is fulfilled.'

Salim Effendi paced back and forth in that room, the signs of humanity apparent in his homely features, as he repeated, in tones that harmonized with the meows of cats over bones, the verse of Abu'l-'Ala' al-Ma'arri:

> Although I be the latest in regard to time,
> I perform what none of the ancients can equal.

After an hour, our friend was prostrate in his rumpled clothes on his disheveled bed. His snoring filled the air of that quarter with strains closer to the creaking of a mill wheel than to the voice of a human being.

POET

A ring connecting this world to the next. A sweet spring from which thirsty souls draw water. A firmly planted tree on the bank of the river of beauty, on which grow ripe fruits sought by ravenous hearts. A nightingale that perches on the bough of speech and warbles melodies that fill the inner souls of predators with kindness and tenderness. A white cloud that appears above the horizon, then expands and ascends until it fills the entire visage of the heavens and rains down to water the flowers of life's field. An angel whom the gods dispatched to teach the people divine things. A radiant light that the darkness does not vanquish and the bushel does not hide, which Astarte, the goddess of love, filled with oil and Apollo, the god of music, kindled.

A solitary figure who arrays himself in simplicity, dines on grace, sits with nature learning to innovate, and keeps vigil in the quiet of the night, awaiting the descent of the spirit. A planter who sows, in the garden of defamation, the kernels of his heart, which produce a plentiful crop that humanity exploits and eats.

This is the poet, of whom the people remain ignorant while he is alive, but whom they recognize when he bids farewell to this world and returns to his celestial homeland. He it is who seeks from humankind only a tiny smile, whose breaths ascend, filling the heavens with living, exquisite apparitions, and whom the people begrudge a crust of bread and a place to lay his head.

How long, humankind, how long O world, will you raise buildings to honor those who made a new crust for the earth out of gore, while you neglect those who bestow upon you their virtues, both when they greet you and when they part from you? How long will you extol those killed and those who bend their necks beneath the yoke of enslavement, yet ignore those who pour out light from their pupils in the dark of night to teach you to see the glory of day and who spend their lives caught in the talons of misfortune so that the pleasure of happiness might not escape you?

And you, poets, life of this life: You have triumphed over the centuries, despite the cruelty of the eons; and you have won the crown away from the haughty, despite the thorns of arrogance; you have taken possession of the hearts, and your dominion knows no end or cessation, O poets.

THE HUSK AND
THE PITH

I never drank the cup of bitterness save that I found its lees to be honey.

I never ascended a narrow pass save that I reached a green sward.

I never lost a friend in the mists of the heavens save that I found him in the clarity of dawn.

How many are the times that I concealed my pain and burning beneath the cloak of resignation, imagining that therein lay recompense and righteousness. But when I threw off that mantle, I saw that the pain had changed to elation and the burning had been transformed into coolness and peace.

How many are the times that I walked with my friend in the world of appearances, muttering to myself about his foolishness and stupidity. But I never arrived at the world of mysteries until I discovered myself to be an overbearing tyrant and found him to be witty and wise.

How many are the times that I became drunk with the wine of self, and considered myself and my companion to be

lamb and wolf, yet when I sobered up from my intoxication
I saw that I was a human being and he was a human being.

You and I, O people, are trapped by the surface appearances
of our situation, veiled from the unseen essence of our reality.
Should any among us stumble, we say he is fallen; and if he
slackens his pace, we say he is old and decrepit; and if he
stammers, we say he is mute; and if he sighs, we say it is his
death rattle, and he is dying.

You and I are infatuated with the husk of 'I' and the
superficialities of 'you.' For this reason, we do not perceive
what the spirit has confided to 'I,' and what it has ensconced
in 'you.'

What can we do, when our arrogance makes us heedless
of the truth that lies within us?

I say to you – though perhaps my words are a veil, cloaking
the face of my reality – I say to you and to my own soul that
what we see with our eyes is no more than a cloud that hides
from us what we must perceive by insight. What we hear
with our ears is only a clangor that distorts what we must
comprehend by our hearts. If we witness the police leading
a man to prison, we must avoid pronouncing either of them
the criminal. If we see a man stained with his own blood,
and another whose hands are dyed red, we must abstain from
judging which is the murderer and which the victim. If we
hear a man singing while another conducts, let us be patient
while we establish which one is really the entertainer.

No, my brother, do not make inferences about the reality
of a man on the basis of appearances, and do not take some
saying or some deed of his as a token of his innermost essence.

Many a person you consider ignorant – because he lacks eloquence or speaks in a colorless tone – has an awareness that leads to wisdom and a heart that serves as a cradle of revelation. And many a person you despise because of repulsive features or a vile livelihood nevertheless was a gift from heaven and a breath from God.

You might visit a palace and a hovel on the same day, exiting the first in awe and the second in pity; but if you could pierce the appearances woven by your senses, your awe would wane and descend to the slough of regret, and your pity would be transformed and ascend to the rank of veneration.

You might encounter between your morning and your evening two men. The first speaks to you, the song of a storm in his voice, a martial intimidation in his gestures. As for the second, he engages you in conversation, fearful, timorous, his voice wavering and his words disjointed. You impute resolve and valor to the first and frailty and spinelessness to the second. But if you were to see them at a time when the days had summoned them to meet tribulations, or to suffer martyrdom for the sake of principle, you would discover that brazen impudence is not bravery and quiet shyness is not cowardice.

You might look out from the window of your house and see among the passersby a nun walking to the right and a harlot walking to the left. You say, immediately, 'How noble is the one, and how disgusting the other!' But if you closed your eyes and listened for a brief moment, you would hear a voice whispering in the ether, saying, 'This one seeks Me

[73]

through her prayers and that one beseeches Me by her anguish, and in the spirit of each is a shadow of My own Spirit.'

You might roam the earth searching for what you term civilization and progress. You enter a city of skyscrapers, with magnificent public buildings and wide avenues. The people therein scurry here and there: This one tunnels through the earth and that one soars into the sky; one unsheathes lightning while another carries out atmospheric research. All of them are attired in tailor-made clothes of unique design, as though they are celebrating a holy day or festival.

After a few days you reach another city, with humble dwellings, amid narrow alleyways, which become in a downpour of rain islands of clay in a sea of mud. In the glare of the sun they are transformed into clouds of dust. As for its residents, they still occupy the space between naturalness and simplicity, like a string hanging between two nocks of a bow. They walk slowly, work sluggishly, and gaze at you as if behind their pupils are another set of eyes, staring at something far distant from you. You depart from their city filled with loathing and disgust, saying to yourself, 'The difference between what I saw in the first city and in the second is like the difference between life and death. The first was all power and expansiveness, the second all weakness and ebb. The first possessed the diligence of spring and summer, the second the lassitude of fall and winter. The first was, in its vigor, a youth dancing in a garden; the second, in its feebleness, an antique tossed upon the ashes.'

If the eye, however, could look by the light of God upon the two cities, it would see them as two trees of the same sort standing in the same orchard. A clear-sighted view of their reality might be given to you, and you would see that what you considered advancement in one was only ephemeral, glistening bubbles. And what you considered languor in the other was an invisible, enduring essence.

No, life is not on the surface, but hidden, and the visible world lies not in its husk but in its pith. People are summed up not by their faces but by their hearts.

Nor is a religion the sum of its outward manifestations, such as its edifices, its rituals, and its traditions, but rather it lies in what souls harbor and in the intentions they form.

The essence of art is not the high notes or the low notes of songs, or the ringing of words in an ode, or the lines and hues of a picture that you see with your eyes. Rather, art lies in the silent, pulsating intervals between the high notes and the low notes. It lies in the feeling that steals into you from listening to an ode, a feeling that remains hushed, quiet, and alone in the spirit of the poet. It lies in the picture's revelation to you, so that you see, while you are gazing at it, what transcends and is more beautiful than it.

No, my brother, days and nights are not their outward appearances, and I – I who am walking in the pageant of days and nights – am not these words that I cast before you, except insofar as these words convey to you something of my silent interiority. Do not reckon me ignorant, then, before you probe my hidden essence, and do not imagine me a genius before you strip me of this acquired essence. Do not say, 'He is a grasping miser,' before you see my heart, or 'He is noble and generous,' before you know what inspires me to nobility and generosity. Call me not a lover until my love manifests itself to you with all the light and fire it holds within it, and call me not carefree until you touch my bleeding wound.

FLOWER SONG

I am a word spoken by nature, which nature retrieves and shrouds within its heart, then utters again. I am a star that has plummeted from the blue canopy upon green leas.

I am the daughter of the elements, with which winter was impregnated and spring brought forth; and summer nurtured; and autumn put to sleep.

I am the gift of lovers; I am the diadem of the bride; I am the last present of the living to the dead.

At the break of day I collude with the breezes in announcing the advent of light, and in the evening I join the birds in bidding it farewell.

I billow upon the plains and embellish them, I breathe the air and perfume it. I embrace sleep, and the myriad eyes of night stare at me; I seek wakefulness, that I might gaze upon the solitary eye of day.

I drink the wine of dew, listen to the songs of thrushes, and dance to the applause of the grasses. I ever look upward, that I might see the light rather than my own fantasies; and this is a wisdom that humans have not yet learned.

VISION

Youth walked before me and I followed his lead until, when we arrived at a distant field, he halted. He contemplated the clouds hurrying above the horizon like a flock of white ewes and the trees that gestured with unadorned branches toward the lofty heights, as though beseeching the heavens to restore their lush foliage. I said, 'Where are we, youth?'

He said, 'In the fields of bewilderment, so beware.'

I said, 'Let us return! The isolation of this place frightens me, and the spectacle of the clouds and naked trees depresses my soul.'

'Be patient. Bewilderment is the beginning of knowledge.'

Then I looked and, behold, there stood a houri approaching us like a fantasy. I shouted in amazement, 'Who is that?'

He said, 'She is Melpomene, the daughter of Jupiter, the mistress of tragedy.'

I said, 'What does tragedy want of me, when you are standing next to me and spreading good cheer?'

He said, 'She came to show you the earth and its woes, for whoso does not see travails can never gaze on joy.'

The houri put her hand over my eyes. When she lifted it I saw myself separated from my youth and abstracted from the robes of matter. I said, 'Where is youth, O daughter of the gods?'

She gave no answer. Rather, she embraced me with her wings and flew with me to the summit of a towering mountain, and I saw the earth and everything on it stretched out before me like a leaf of a book. And the secrets of its inhabitants were as manifest to me as the lines on a page. I stood in awe next to the houri, meditating upon the secrets of humankind, seeking an answer to the riddles of life. I saw, and would that I had not seen! I saw the angels of happiness battle the demons of misery, while human beings stood between them in a perplexity that inclined them sometimes toward hope and sometimes toward despair. I saw love and malice toying with the human heart: The one veils the sins of human beings and makes them drunk with the wine of subservience, loosening their tongues in praise and commendation, while the other inflames their enmities, blinds them to reality, and stops their ears from hearing true words. I saw the city sitting, like a street girl clutching at the hems of the son of man, then I saw the beautiful countryside standing at a distance and weeping for her sake.

I saw the priests resort to artifice like foxes, false messiahs seizing control of the souls' inclinations, while humanity cries out for help from wisdom, who despises it, nursing a violent anger toward it, because it ignored her when she called to it in public, on the streets. I saw the clerics multiply their heavenward glances while their hearts were interred in the crypts of greed. I saw youths profess love with their lips and draw nigh to their hopes of frivolity, while their divinity remained distant and their feelings slumbered. I saw the religiously observant trading in gossip in the bazaar of betrayal and hypocrisy, and the doctors playing with the souls of simple, trusting folk. I saw the ignorant accepted into the company of the wise. This fool represented his past as a throne of glory, bestowed on his present a cushion of affluence, and rolled out for his future the carpet of magnificence. I saw impoverished wretches sowing while the rich and powerful reaped and ate, as inequity stood there, labelled by the people 'the holy law.' I saw thieves in the dark stealing the riches of the mind while the guardians of the light drowned in the sleep of lassitude. I saw woman as a lute in the hands of a man who played her poorly, so she produced melodies that did not please him. I saw those familiar phalanxes besieging the city of inherited honor, but I saw phalanxes that were routed because they were few and disunited. I saw true liberty walking the streets and standing at thresholds begging for refuge, and the people turning her away. Then I saw degradation moving in a great procession, and the people calling it liberty. I saw religion buried in the depths of a book while delusions took its place. I saw human beings condemn patience as cowardice, label forbearance laziness, and call kindness fear. I saw intruders at the table of good manners put on airs, while the invited guests remained silent. I saw wealth as a web of iniquity in the hands of a wastrel and as a motive for the people's hatred in the hands of a miser; and in the hands of a sage I never saw wealth.

When I had witnessed all these things, I cried out in anguish from that lookout, 'Is this the earth, daughter of the gods?'

She replied in a quiet voice that cut to the quick, 'This is the path of the self, strewn with thorns and ghouls. This is the shadow of the human. This is the night, and dawn will yet break.'

Then she put her hand over my eyes, and when she removed it I discovered myself and my youth ambling along, while hope sprinted before me.

MY SOUL GAVE ME
GOOD COUNSEL

My soul gave me good counsel, teaching me to love what the people abhor and to show good will toward the one they hate. It showed me that love is a property not of the lover but of the beloved. Before my soul taught me, love was for me a delicate thread stretched between two adjacent pegs, but now it has been transformed into a halo; its first is its last, and its last is its first. It encompasses every being, slowly expanding to embrace all that ever will be.

*   *   *

My soul gave me good counsel, teaching me to find the beauty concealed in a face, a color, a complexion, and to gaze intently at what the people think ugly, until it shows me its comeliness. Before my soul taught me, I saw beauty as quivering flames between pillars of smoke; but it faded and I no longer see anything but the kindling that bursts into flame.

*   *   *

My soul gave me good counsel, teaching me to listen to the voices not produced by tongues, nor shouted from throats. Before my soul taught me, my ears were weary and ailing, and I was conscious only of uproar and discord. Now I sip at silence and listen to its inwardness that chants songs of the eons, reciting praises of the sky, announcing the mysteries of the Unseen.

*　*　*

My soul gave me good counsel, teaching me to drink what has not been squeezed or poured into cups, what is not raised by the hands nor touched by the lips. Before my soul taught me, my thirst was a faint spark in a mound of ash, which I would quench with water from a pool or with a sip of freshly squeezed juice. Now, however, my yearning is my cup, my burning thirst is my drink, and my solitude is my intoxication; I do not and shall not quench my thirst. But in this burning that is never extinguished is a joy that never wanes.

*　*　*

My soul gave me good counsel, teaching me to touch what has never taken corporeal form or crystallized. It made me understand that touching something is half the task of comprehending it, and that what we grasp therein is part of what we desire from it. Before my soul taught me, I contented myself with heat when cold, and with cold when hot, and with either if I was listless. But now my once-cramped sense of touch is scattered everywhere, having metamorphosed

into a fine mist that penetrates everything that appears from Being, so as to mingle with what has remained hidden from it.

* * *

My soul gave me good counsel, teaching me to smell the fragrances that neither aromatic herb nor incense has diffused abroad. Before my soul taught me, whenever I craved a scent I sought it in gardens or in perfume bottles or censers. But now I have begun to smell what does not burn or spill, and I fill my chest with pure breaths that have never passed through a garden in this world and have never been carried aloft by a breeze belonging to this sky.

* * *

My soul gave me good counsel, teaching me to say, 'Here I am!' when the unknown and the perilous call me. Before my soul taught me, I refused to arise save for the voice of a caller I recognized, and I never fared upon any ways save those I had tried and found easy. Now the known has become my mount, which I ride toward the unknown, and the level plain has become my stairs, whose steps I ascend to put myself in jeopardy.

* * *

My soul gave me good counsel, teaching me not to measure time by saying, 'It was yesterday, and will be tomorrow.' Before my soul taught me, I imagined the past as an era not to be met with, and the future as an age that I would never witness. But now I know that in the brief moment of the present, all time exists, including everything that is in time – all that is eagerly anticipated, achieved, or realized.

* * *

My soul gave me good counsel, teaching me not to define a place by saying 'here' or 'there.' Before my soul taught me, I thought that when I was in any place on the earth I was remote from every other spot. But now I have learned that the place where I subsist is all places, and the space I occupy is all intervals.

* * *

My soul gave me good counsel, teaching me to stay up late while the inhabitants of the quarter slumber, and to sleep while they are awake. Before my soul taught me, I never experienced their dreams while unconscious, and they never shared my dreams in their heedlessness. But now I only swim, arms fluttering, in my sleep with them as my companions, and they do not soar in their dreams save that I rejoice in their liberation.

* * *

My soul gave me good counsel, teaching me never to delight in praise or to be distressed by reproach. Before my soul taught me, I doubted the value of my accomplishments until the passing days sent someone who would extol or disparage them. But now I know that trees blossom in the spring and give their fruits in the summer without any desire for accolades. And they scatter their leaves abroad in the fall and denude themselves in the winter without fear of reproof.

*   *   *

My soul gave me good counsel, teaching me and demonstrating to me that I am not exalted over the panhandler nor less than the mighty. Before my soul taught me, I thought people consisted of two types: the weak, whom I pitied and disregarded, and the powerful, whom I followed or against whom I rebelled. Now, I have discovered that I was formed as one individual from the same substance from which all human beings were created. I am made up of the same elements as they are, and my pattern is theirs. My struggles are theirs, and my path is theirs. If they do wrong, I am culpable, and if they perform a good deed, I am proud of their act. If they arise, I arise with them, and if they remain seated, so do I.

*   *   *

My soul gave me good counsel, teaching me that the lamp which I carry does not belong to me, and the song that I sing was not generated from within me. Even if I walk with light, I am not the light; and if I am a taut-stringed lute, I am not the lute player.

*   *   *

My soul gave me good counsel, my friend, and taught me. Your soul, too, has given you good counsel, and taught you. You and I are similar and alike, and the only difference between us is that I speak of what is within me and my speech is somewhat insistent, whereas you conceal what is within you, and from your restraint shines forth the face of virtue.

PERFECTION

You ask me, my brother, when humankind will attain perfection.

Listen to my reply:

Humankind will proceed toward perfection when it feels that humanity is: A limitless sky and a shoreless ocean, an ever-blazing flame, an eternally gleaming light, a wind when it gusts and when it is calm, a cloud when it thunders and lightnings and rains, a stream when it sings or roars, a tree when it blossoms in the spring and disrobes in the autumn, a mountain when it towers, a valley when it descends, and a field when it is fertile or barren.

When humankind has felt all these things, it will have reached the midway point in its path toward perfection. If it wishes to arrive at the road to perfection, it must, if it perceives its own essence, feel that humanity is: an infant relying on its mother, a mature man responsible for his dependants, a youth lost among his desires and his passions, an elderly man whose past and future wrestle with one another, a worshipper in his hermitage, a criminal in his cell, a scholar amidst his books and papers, a fool between the black of night and the dark of his day, a nun among the flowers of her faith and the thorns of her loneliness, a prostitute between the talons of her weakness and the claws of her neediness, the indigent between his bitterness and complaisance, the rich man between his ambitions and his submission, the poet between the fog of his evenings and the rays of his dawns.

Should humankind prove able to experience and know all these things, it will arrive at perfection and become one shadow among the shadows of God.

THE BEAUTY OF DEATH
Dedicated to M.E.H.

Leave me, all of you. For my soul is drunk with love.

Let me sleep, for my spirit is satiated with days and nights.

Light the candles and incense around my bed, scatter rose and narcissus petals on my body, anoint my hair with pressed musk, sprinkle perfume on my feet, then look, and read what the hand of death has inscribed upon my brow.

Leave me to drown in the arms of slumber, for my eyelids have wearied of this wakefulness.

Strum upon lutes and let the ringing of their silver strings pulsate in my ears.

Blow on reed flutes and weave from their sweet melodies a shroud about my heart, which is hastening toward a standstill.

Sing tranquil songs and from their enchanted meanings spread out a carpet for my feelings, then contemplate and gaze upon the ray of hope in my eyes.

Wipe away the tears, my friends, and raise your heads the way flowers lift their crowns at the approach of dawn, and look upon the bride of death standing like a column of light between my bed and the sky . . . Hold your breaths and listen one brief moment, strive to hear with me the rustling of her white wings.

Come and take your leave of me, children of my mother! Kiss my forehead with smiling lips. Kiss my lips with your eyelids, and kiss my eyelids with your lips.

Bring the children near my bed and let them touch my neck with their tender, pink fingers. Gather round the elderly so that they may bless my brow with their hardened, wizened hands. Let the girls of the quarter approach and see God's likeness in my eyes and hear the echo of infinite songs in the breaths I take.

FAREWELL

Behold, I have reached the peak of the mountain and my spirit has taken flight in the heavens of freedom and liberation.

I have gone far, far away, O children of my mother; the hills beyond the mists are now hidden from my view, the last traces of the valleys have been flooded by the ocean of serenity, and the paths and trails have been erased by the hand of oblivion. The meadows, forests, and mountain passes are masked by phantasms that are white as spring clouds, yellow as sunbeams, and red as dusk's sash.

The roar of ocean waves has faded, the purling of brooks in the fields has ceased, the voices of the crowd have dissipated, and I no longer hear anything but the anthem of eternity, which harmonizes with the desires of the spirit.

REST

Remove the linen fabric from my body and enshroud me in jasmine and iris petals. Deliver my remains from the ivory coffin, and stretch them out upon pillows of orange and lemon blossoms. Sing me no dirges, O children of my mother. Rather, sing out the songs of youth and joy. Shed no tears, daughter of the fields. Rather, chant the lyrics of harvesting and pressing.

Do not cover my breast with your moans and sighs. Rather, trace upon it with your fingertips the runes of love and the emblems of joy.

Do not disturb the repose of the ether with rites and incantations. Rather, call upon hearts to sing praises with me of immortality and eternity.

Wear not black out of sorrow for me but, rather, put on white, rejoicing with me.

Speak not of my death with a lump in your throats. Rather, close your eyes and you will see me among you, now, tomorrow, and thereafter.

Lay me out upon leafy branches, lift me upon your shoulders, and carry me slowly to the open country.

Do not convey me to the cemetery, for the crowding will disturb my peace and the rattling of bones and skulls will deprive my resting place of quietude.

Carry me to the cypress grove and dig my grave in that spot where violets grow next to anemones.

Dig a deep grave, lest floodwaters carry my bones down into the valley.

Dig a wide grave, that the night specters might come and sit beside it.

Remove these clothes and lower me naked into the bosom of the earth. Stretch me out slowly, quietly upon the breast of my mother.

Cover me with soft earth, and with every shovelful throw in a handful of lily, jasmine, and wild rose seeds, that they might grow over my grave, imbibing the elements of my body, diffusing in the air the fragrance of my heart, lifting up to the sun's countenance the mysteries of my repose. And as they bow with the breeze, may they remind passersby of my past dreams and aspirations.

Leave me now, children of my mother, leave me alone and walk with mute feet, as silence prowls secluded valleys.

Leave me alone and disperse from my side noiselessly, just as almond and apple blossoms scatter before April breezes.

Return to your homes and you will discover there what death cannot steal from me or from you.

Leave this place, for the one you seek has grown remote, very remote from this world.

THE LETTERS OF FIRE

Engrave on my tombstone:
'Here lies one whose name was writ in water.'
John Keats

Do the nights thus pass us by? Do they thus wrap themselves in their mantles beneath the feet of time? Do the centuries in this manner fold us up, preserving nothing of us save a name that they etch upon their scrolls with water rather than ink?

Will this light be extinguished? This love vanish? These hopes wane? Shall death demolish all that we build? The wind disperse all that we say? The shadow obscure all that we do?

Is this truly life? Is it a past that has faded, the traces of which have disappeared; a present that scurries to catch up to the past; a future without meaning, save when it passes by, becoming present or past? Will all the joys of our hearts and the sorrows of our souls evaporate without our knowing their repercussions?

Are human beings, then, like sea foam that wells up for a moment on the water's surface, only to be quelled by a stiff wind, so that it is as if it had never existed?

No, by my life! For the reality of life is life. Life never began in the womb and shall never end in the charnel house.

These years are naught but an instant in an everlasting, unceasing life. This worldly life with all that it contains is a dream beside the awakening that we term death the terrible. A dream, but all that we see and do therein will live forever in God's eternity.

The æther bears every smile and every sigh that ascends from our hearts, preserving the murmur of every kiss that originated in love. The angels enumerate every tear shed by grief from our eyes, and fill the ears of the spirits that sing praises in the limitless void with all the songs that joy composed from our feelings.

There in the next world we shall see all the highs and lows of our emotional lives and the throbbing of our hearts. There we shall perceive the substance of our divinity, which now we revile, driven as we are by despair.

The error that we today call weakness will appear tomorrow as a link in its being, necessary for completing the chain of human life.

The drudgery for which we are not recompensed now will live with us and announce our glory.

The burdens that we now bear will be diadems of honor.

If Keats, that warbling nightingale, had known that his songs would still be spreading the love of beauty in the hearts of men and women, he would have said,

> Engrave on my tombstone: 'Here are the remains of one who wrote his name across the sky with letters of fire.'

THE REALM OF
HAPPINESS

My heart wearied within me, until it bade me farewell and journeyed to the Realm of Happiness in the next world. When it arrived at that shrine sanctified by the soul, it stood bewildered, for it did not witness there what it had for so long envisioned. It saw not power, wealth, or sovereignty. It saw only the youth of beauty; his consort, the daughter of love; and their child, wisdom.

My heart addressed the daughter of love, saying, 'Where is contentment, Love? For I have heard that the inhabitants of this place partake thereof.'

She replied, 'Contentment has gone to preach in the city of overweening ambition, for we have no need of her. Happiness does not seek contentment; rather, happiness is a yearning that is embraced by union, whereas contentment is a forgetfulness assailed by oblivion. The immortal soul is never contented, for it desires perfection, and perfection is infinity.'

My heart addressed the youth of beauty, saying, 'Reveal to me the mystery of woman, Beauty, and enlighten me, for you are knowledge.'

He replied, 'She is you, the human heart, and whatever describes you describes her. She and I are one, and wherever I alight she descends. She is like religion uncorrupted by the ignorant, like a moon not veiled by clouds, like a breeze unadulterated by the breaths of depravity.'

My heart approached Wisdom, the daughter of Love and Beauty, and said, 'Give me wisdom, that I may convey it to humanity.'

She replied, 'It is happiness, which begins in the soul's holiest of holies and never comes from without.'

READ MORE IN PENGUIN

In every corner of the world, on every subject under the sun, Penguin represents quality and variety – the very best in publishing today.

For complete information about books available from Penguin – including Puffins, Penguin Classics and Arkana – and how to order them, write to us at the appropriate address below. Please note that for copyright reasons the selection of books varies from country to country.

In the United Kingdom: Please write to *Dept. EP, Penguin Books Ltd, Bath Road, Harmondsworth, West Drayton, Middlesex UB7 ODA*

In the United States: Please write to *Consumer Sales, Penguin USA, P.O. Box 999, Dept. 17109, Bergenfield, New Jersey 07621-0120.* VISA and MasterCard holders call 1-800-253-6476 to order Penguin titles

In Canada: Please write to *Penguin Books Canada Ltd, 10 Alcorn Avenue, Suite 300, Toronto, Ontario M4V 3B2*

In Australia: Please write to *Penguin Books Australia Ltd, P.O. Box 257, Ringwood, Victoria 3134*

In New Zealand: Please write to *Penguin Books (NZ) Ltd, Private Bag 102902, North Shore Mail Centre, Auckland 10*

In India: Please write to *Penguin Books India Pvt Ltd, 706 Eros Apartments, 56 Nehru Place, New Delhi 110 019*

In the Netherlands: Please write to *Penguin Books Netherlands bv, Postbus 3507, NL-1001 AH Amsterdam*

In Germany: Please write to *Penguin Books Deutschland GmbH, Metzlerstrasse 26, 60594 Frankfurt am Main*

In Spain: Please write to *Penguin Books S. A., Bravo Murillo 19, 1° B, 28015 Madrid*

In Italy: Please write to *Penguin Italia s.r.l., Via Felice Casati 20, I–20124 Milano*

In France: Please write to *Penguin France S. A., 17 rue Lejeune, F–31000 Toulouse*

In Japan: Please write to *Penguin Books Japan, Ishikiribashi Building, 2–5–4, Suido, Bunkyo-ku, Tokyo 112*

In South Africa: Please write to *Longman Penguin Southern Africa (Pty) Ltd, Private Bag X08, Bertsham 2013*

NEW AGE BOOKS FOR MIND, BODY & SPIRIT

BY THE SAME AUTHOR

The Prophet

The Prophet is the most famous work of religious inspiration of the twentieth century. Translated into more than twenty languages, it is a treasury of counsel on human life, and has given uplift and balm to millions around the world.

The Garden of the Prophet

Published posthumously in 1933, *The Garden of the Prophet* is the book Gibran was working on in the years leading up to his untimely death. Full of insights expressed in Gibran's unique style on the nature of wisdom, time, loneliness and God, it resonates with the humanity and compassion of its author on every page.

The Prophet, read by Renu Setna, and *The Garden of the Prophet*, read by Nadim Sawalha, are also available as Penguin Audiobooks.

The Storm
Stories and Prose Poems

Four stories and prose poems, *The Storm* gives definitive expression to many of Gibran's key themes. This important new translation adds a fresh dimension to our understanding of his whole philosophy and career.

The Beloved
Reflections on the Path of the Heart

A selection of exquisite writings on love, marriage and the spiritual union of souls.

also published:

Jesus the Son of Man
The Voice of Kahlil Gibran
An anthology edited by Robin Waterfield